olens

IZENSHIP

1

THE

OUTBURST!

Mike Gould

Playscripts and drama for CPSHE

United Kingdom: Folens Publishers, Apex Business Centre, Boscombe Road, Dunstable, LU5 4RL.
Email: folens@folens.com

Ireland: Folens Publishers, Greenhills Road, Tallaght, Dublin 24.
Email: info@folens.ie

Poland: JUKA, ul. Renesansowa 38, Warsaw 01-905.

Editor: Kay Macmullan

Layout artist: Suzanne Ward

Cover design: Martin Cross

First published 2003 by Folens Limited.

Every effort has been made to trace the copyright holders of material used in this publication. If any copyright holder has been overlooked, we should be pleased to make any necessary arrangements.

British Library Cataloguing in Publication Data. A catalogue record for this publication is available from the British Library.

ISBN 1 84303 532 4

Contents

Introduction

The plays in this collection, *The Media World* are designed for use in a conventional classroom, as read-round plays, or can be performed in a drama studio or acting space. They have been written so that they work as real dramas, not just as written texts for study, and to that end they are flexible enough to be used, should you or your students choose, as performed pieces in assemblies, or in front of other classes as part of Citizenship work related to media issues. However, there is no expectation that they are presented like this, and no teacher using them will require drama-teaching expertise.

Realistically, it is most likely that the plays will be read around a class or group. However, it is recommended that someone (either yourself, or a student) reads the stage directions aloud. For example, a play such as *The first casualty* is particularly dependent on different scenes and locations.

The plays themselves vary in degrees of complexity and length, although it is fair to say that the earlier plays (i.e. the first three or four in the book) are probably more accessible and lighter in tone and subject matter. The two most challenging plays in terms of subject matter are probably *The truth about Gina* and *The first casualty*. The former was the first play I wrote for this collection and, in a sense, sets the tone for the others. It is about perspective, how we can believe what we are told, and what messages the media convey, all set within a personal context affecting people's everyday lives. It is partly based on real events, though the names and details have been significantly changed. *The first casualty*, the last play in the collection, deals with the press in a more positive light, and looks at the process of 'embedding' (the way in which reporters' access to news is controlled by the military who protect them).

Each play provides basic stage directions, and a character list, and at the back of the book there are brief teacher's notes for each play proposing some discussion points and referring the teacher to aspects of the Citizenship curriculum most suited to the play.

In the end, however, the plays have been designed neither to preach nor to moralise. My task as writer of these plays and of the others in this series, was to create living, powerful dramas that work as good stories. The issues arise out of the decisions and situations characters have to face, not the other way round.

I hope you find the plays stimulating and enjoyable.

Mike Gould

The news according to Ben

Characters

BEN: Ben Baker, aged 13

HOLLY: Holly Baker, his sister, aged 14–15

JOE: Joe Ridgely, Ben's friend

MRS BAKER: Holly and Ben's mother (non-speaking part)

Scene 1

Ben's bedroom, which doubles as a TV studio.

BEN speaks as a newsreader by sitting on the edge of his bed facing the audience. There should be a bedroom door to one side of the stage or acting space.

BEN: This is the news at six with me, Ben Baker. And here are the headlines.

JOE is cradling an electric guitar and plays a suitably dramatic chord. Next to him, but somewhat out of the picture, is Ben's older sister, HOLLY.

BEN: Baker narrowly fails to make school football team.

JOE plays same chord.

BEN: Baker grounded for getting two detentions in one week.

JOE plays chord.

BEN: Dad's stir-fry OK but not up to standard of mum's, say experts. And, showbiz news … (*holding up picture of Holly*) Holly Baker comes third in Talent Show. (*picks up sheets of paper from beside him on the bed*) And now for the news in detail … Ben Baker's late miss in front of an open goal in today's footie trials seems certain to have cost him a place in the school team. Over to Joe Ridgley who is on the spot.

JOE is wearing a long overcoat. HOLLY is holding a hair dryer, which is blowing JOE's hair about.

JOE: Here, on a windy afternoon at Blackwood High School, we have just seen Ben Baker's attempts at selection for the school team disappear into the mud. With just two minutes to go, and the teams locked at 0–0, Ben was put through with only the goalkeeper to beat, but as he drew his foot back to shoot, he slipped and fell flat on his face, and the chance was gone … now back to the studio.

BEN: Err, isn't there something else to add?

JOE: Oh, yes. However, it seems highly probable that at some stage, Baker's sublime skills will get him into the team and that the bad luck that has dogged his career …

HOLLY: Bad luck? Huh!

JOE: … dogged his career, will come to an end. Now, back to the studio.

BEN: Thank you, Joe. Joe Ridgley there at Blackwood High.

Knock on door. JOE opens it. MRS BAKER marches in with a piece of paper and thrusts it into BEN's hands. She looks cross.

BEN: And we have to interrupt this bulletin for some urgent news. (*reads note*) Ben Baker's plans for an evening of pizza and DVDs have been cruelly dashed by the news that he has to wash his football boots, and catch up on the two pieces of homework his mother has discovered in his school bag. There may be an update on that story later this evening, but for now, this is Ben Baker saying 'goodnight' from the Baker Studios. Goodnight!

HOLLY: What about my Talent Show story?

JOE: Yeah, and you didn't even mention my new band. We've got our first gig.

BEN: School assembly? It's hardly Glastonbury, is it?

HOLLY: Everyone's got to start somewhere. So, how come you didn't mention my third place?

BEN: The news has to adapt according to changing circumstances.

HOLLY: What?

JOE: Huh?

BEN: You saw Mum's face. If a big news story comes in, then you sometimes have to ditch the others.

JOE: Yeah, but who decides what's the big story?

BEN: I do.

HOLLY: That's not fair.

BEN: I know. But decisions have to be made. The news happens too quickly. We can't have a committee deciding what goes in and what doesn't.

JOE: Why not? You could for the main stories. I mean, fair enough if a big story comes in during the news.

BEN: That's what happened.

HOLLY: Yeah, but it involved you. Surely it needs someone a bit more …

JOE: … objective. You know, not involved.

HOLLY: *All* the stories are about you.

BEN: What about the Talent Show story?

HOLLY: You didn't do it!

BEN: I mentioned it in the headlines.

HOLLY: Yeah, but then you didn't give any details.

BEN: I was going to.

HOLLY: Right! Course you were. Well, I quit.

BEN: What as?

HOLLY: Exactly. I don't even know what my job is. I bet Trevor McDonald doesn't have this problem. I bet he doesn't have to check if he's 'Chief Holder of Hair Dryer' or 'Newsreader'.

JOE: Yeah. I quit too.

BEN: You can't quit! You're my main reporter.

JOE: Your *only* reporter. Sorry, mate, if you can't run this news programme properly then we're going elsewhere.

BEN: Elsewhere? What d'you mean?

HOLLY: I hear Jodie Hughes has started her own show.

BEN: What's it called?

HOLLY: Hughes at 43.

BEN: 43?

JOE: That's the number of her house.

HOLLY: And there's a hospitality suite.

BEN: A what?

JOE: The kitchen. You get Coke and crisps. McCoys.

JOE and HOLLY get up and start to leave. JOE takes his guitar.

BEN: Oi, you two. Wait!

HOLLY: Too late. We've had a better offer. Come on, Joe (*she takes him by the hand*)

BEN: Joe, what's she doing?

JOE: Can't you see? Could have been in the celebrity slot. Joe Ridgley and Holly Baker start dating.

JOE and HOLLY leave.

BEN slumps back on to his bed. He picks up remote and flips on the TV (out of view of audience).

TREVOR
MCDONALD: And the main news tonight. Baker TV, the up-and-coming news channel was sensationally taken off air tonight as the reporters went on strike, and then defected to rival channel Hughes News. Boss of Baker TV, Ben Baker, was said to be distraught at the news, and admitted he hadn't seen it coming. This is the most recent in a long line of disappointments for Baker, starting with his failure to get into the school soccer team after he …

BEN *(switching off TV)*:
Oh, shut up, McDonald!

Scene 2

Ben's bedroom.

JOE and HOLLY sitting on edge of bed. BEN in chair or bean-bag to one side.

HOLLY: So, these are our conditions …

BEN: You've already told me.

JOE: Well, we're telling you again. So there's no confusion.

BEN *(sighs)*: All right. I'm listening.

HOLLY: Right. First, you have little editorial control over what goes into the news. By all means you can contribute to the discussion.

BEN: Discussion?

HOLLY: Yes. An hour before we shoot the news we all sit down and sift through the news stories. You know, prioritise them. Then, if any late news comes in, we adapt them before we go on air.

BEN: OK. Agreed.

HOLLY: But, as editor and producer, I have the final say.

BEN: What? This is Baker TV. Ben Baker TV.

HOLLY: Well, I'm a Baker, and if you want to survive then these are the terms.

BEN: If I don't?

JOE: Hughes News has made us a very reasonable offer.

BEN: What's in it for you? I mean, staying here?

JOE: I get to be called, 'Home Affairs Correspondent'.

BEN: What about me?

HOLLY: You read the news. You're the face of Baker Ridgley TV.

BEN: Baker Ridgley?!

HOLLY: Seems only fair. After all, Joe is Home Affairs Correspondent. And Foreign Affairs.

BEN: Foreign Affairs?

JOE: Yeah. Remember that holiday I had? I thought I could do something about hotels in Spain.

BEN *(stands up and paces the room)*: I'm not sure …

HOLLY: Well, don't take too long. Hughes News is waiting for our answer.

BEN: OK. I accept.

JOE: Are you sure?

BEN: Yes. I've said so, haven't I?

HOLLY: Well then. Here's your first test.

BEN: What?

JOE: It's nearly six o'clock.

BEN: What about the editorial discussion?

HOLLY: No time for that today. Here are the top stories. (*hands BEN a sheet of paper*) Quick. Get into place. Camera's rolling …

HOLLY and JOE disappear to side. BEN hurriedly sits on edge of bed.

BEN: Welcome to the news at six. And here are today's top stories …

JOE strikes chord on guitar. BEN looks surprised.

BEN *(losing his cool for a moment)*: That sounds different.

JOE: Yeah. I learnt a new one. That's three chords I can play now.

BEN: Sorry for that interruption. The top stories today. New TV channel formed by merger of Baker and Ridgley. Shares slump in Hughes News.

JOE plays chord.

BEN: Holly Baker eyes pop career after success at Talent Show.

JOE plays chord.

BEN: Joe Ridgley named 'Reporter of the Year' following his undercover … undercover?

JOE: Yeah, I spent most of the holiday in bed with food poisoning.

BEN: ... undercover investigation into Spanish hotel food. And finally ... Ben Baker no longer grounded after sister Holly and best mate, Joe, help him with late homework thereby averting detentions … (*suddenly realises what he's just said*) You did what?

JOE: Here, mate. (*hands BEN two exercise books*) Maths and French. Sorted. We felt guilty. Holly did the Maths. Me the French. I'm not called Foreign Affairs Correspondent for nothing.

BEN: And finally … HOLLY: You've done that.

BEN: Well, finally finally … Ben Baker is overcome with emotion at the loyalty of sister and best friend as he faced his darkest hour. That's it for tonight. Goodnight!

HOLLY: Actually, Ben. It wasn't so much loyalty.

BEN: What was it then?

JOE: Jodie Hughes' crisps weren't McCoys.

BEN: They weren't?

JOE: They were those cheap ones from that cash and carry.

HOLLY: Disgusting. Tasted like toilet paper.

JOE: And the Coke was flat.

Blackout.

Without you

Characters

RICKY: aged 13

JULIE: Ricky's sister, aged 15

CARLY: Ricky's sister, aged 9

MUM: Barbara, Ricky's mother

DAD: Colin, Ricky's father

SARA: Sara Taylor, Julie's friend

MRS TAYLOR: Sara's mother

Scene 1

Sitting room.

RICKY enters. He throws school bag to one side and picks up the remote control before slumping down on the sofa. He points the remote at the TV, then stares, open-mouthed at the space where it used to be. He leaps to his feet and rushes over to the spot, then stares around the room. He even picks up a cushion and looks underneath the sofa. Finally, he rushes to the door and calls out …

RICKY: Mum! There's something wrong …

MUM *(enters)*:
What is it? What's the matter? Calm down.

RICKY: It's awful, Mum. Someone's nicked the telly!

MUM: Ah. There's a very simple explanation for this.

RICKY: I know there is. There's been a burglary!

MUM: Not quite.

RICKY *(not listening)*:
This is serious! I mean, the telly.

MUM: It hasn't been stolen.

RICKY: It hasn't?

MUM: No. Not exactly.

RICKY: It's broken? And it was only two months old.

MUM: No, it's fine.

RICKY: Well, what is it, Mum?

MUM: I think you'd better sit down.

RICKY sits down slowly, remote still clutched in his hand.

MUM: I have some bad news.

Scene 2

Same room, a few minutes later.

RICKY pacing round the room.

RICKY: No, Mum. I don't believe it. He wouldn't.

MUM: He has.

RICKY: Does Julie know?

MUM: Yes, she's in her room.

RICKY: Watching her own TV?

MUM: No. That's gone too. And yours.

RICKY: What? This is a nightmare! How could Dad do it?

MUM: You'd better ask him. He'll be home in a minute.

RICKY: We'll soon sort it out, won't we, Mum? He'll see sense. I mean, he's an intelligent man …

MUM *(to herself)*: That's debatable.

RICKY: I mean, a reasonable man.

MUM: No comment.

Scene 3

Kitchen.

Family around the table. RICKY and JULIE are hardly eating. CARLY, the youngest, is eating heartily. It's deathly quiet.

DAD: This is nice. A proper family meal.

MUM: You haven't finished your chips, you two.

CARLY: I'll have them.

JULIE: Go on then. Here. (*tips her chips on to CARLY's plate*)

RICKY: And mine … (*does the same*)

CARLY: Cool! Are you two on hunger strike?

RICKY: No, but that's a good idea.

JULIE: Dad! Why did you have to do it? I mean, all the tellies. Even if you'd left just one.

DAD: It's like being an alcoholic. You have just one … then it all starts again.

MUM: I think that's a bit extreme, Colin.

DAD: Ah ha! That's where you're wrong. I've seen what television has done to this family.

RICKY: Yeah. Keeps us contented and happy in the evenings.

DAD gets out of his chair.

JULIE: Uh oh, here comes a lecture.

DAD: Think of that box. Or should I say boxes? After all, we did have four. Yours and Julie's. The one in the lounge. And the one that used to be in here. That box is like a private brainwashing machine. You stare at it like you're hypnotised. You are drawn to it like a magnet, like bees to the queen bee …

RICKY *(to MUM)*:
What's he on about?

MUM: I think he's trying to say it controls you …

DAD: … like moths to a flame. And like a flame, it burns you.

JULIE: Huh?

DAD: Your minds are damaged. The other day at tea, that soap was on and the only time you turned off was when the news started.

RICKY: See? It doesn't control us. I remember, we started talking.

DAD: Yes, you did. And what did you talk about? TV. Every subject was something from TV. Every person was a character on a TV show or someone who presented a TV show.

JULIE: I think you're exaggerating, Dad.

DAD *(a kind of madness in his eyes)*:
Oh, do you? Do you? (*opens the drawer of the kitchen unit the TV was on, and pulls out a small tape recorder. Presses 'eject' and a cassette springs out*) It's all on here. The proof! Do you want me to play it?

MUM: No, Colin! They believe you, don't you, kids?

JULIE *(to RICKY)*:
He's certainly mad enough.

CARLY *(staring at the cassette)*:
That's my Kylie tape!

DAD: Sorry, darling. I'll get you another.

RICKY: One good thing to come of it, at least.

JULIE: So, Dad, when can we have the tellies back?

DAD: Who knows? Next week? Next month?

RICKY and JULIE exchange horrified looks.

DAD: Maybe never.

RICKY: You wouldn't?

JULIE: You couldn't?

DAD: We'll see. First I want some changes round here.

Scene 4

Kitchen.

RICKY sat at table. There's a newspaper open at the centre spread. MUM enters.

MUM: Hi, love. What are you doing?

RICKY: Reading. The editorial.

MUM: Oh, that's nice. Is it interesting?

RICKY: Are you joking? I don't understand it. At least if it had been on *Newsround* it would have made sense.

MUM: So, why are you persevering?

RICKY: Because it's one of Dad's stupid conditions, if we want the telly back.

MUM: I see. And where's Julie?

RICKY: She's gone round to see Sara.

MUM: She doesn't like Sara. They argued last week at school over some boy.

RICKY: Sara has a wide-screen nicam stereo with a state-of-the art DVD.

MUM: Oh. Does your dad know?

RICKY: I think he suspects something. I saw him watch her leaving. Then he made a phone call.

Scene 5

Sara's house.

SARA and JULIE in sitting room. There's an awkward silence.

SARA: So, how's things?

JULIE: All right.

SARA: To tell the truth, I'm a bit surprised to see you.

JULIE: Yeah, well. Whatever.

SARA: Why are you here?

JULIE: What's the time?

SARA: What?

JULIE: The time?

SARA: Just gone seven. Why?

JULIE: Quick. It's on now.

SARA: What is?

JULIE: *The Simpsons.*

SARA: Right. So, you didn't come round here to make the peace or anything?

JULIE *(not listening)*:
It's started … here, give me that remote. (*goes to switch on the TV, but nothing happens*)

Sara's mother, MRS TAYLOR, comes in.

MRS TAYLOR: Hi, you two. Glad to see you've made it up.

SARA: Don't know that we have.

JULIE: Mrs Taylor, your TV doesn't work.

SARA: Yeah, Mum, what's wrong with it?

MRS TAYLOR: Nothing. It's unplugged. I had a phone call from your father, Julie.

JULIE: What? He wouldn't dare …

MRS TAYLOR: We're old friends, your parents and us.

JULIE: You mean he phoned up and told you that if I came round to watch the telly to stop me?

MRS TAYLOR: I'm afraid so.

SARA: That's why you came round?

JULIE *(looking at her as if she's stupid)*: Hello? Do you really think I'd forgive you for snogging Ben at break? *(gets up)* You parents, you're all the same. Dictators! *(storms out)*

Scene 6

Sitting room.

MUM: Right, everyone, sit down!

DAD: Is this really necessary, Barbara?

MUM: Yes! It is.

The children and Dad sit.

MUM: Right. This TV summit is now officially open.

JULIE: What?

MUM: The meeting. Now, shut up and listen.

DAD: But, dear …

MUM: You too!

RICKY: Way to go, Mum.

MUM: This week has been difficult, to say the least. One: I have had to placate Mary Taylor who was on the phone about a certain person's rudeness.

JULIE: Yeah, Mum. Sorry. I kind of lost it for a moment … it was like, all I could think of was watching my programme.

DAD: Ah ha. Proves my point … just like an addiction.

MUM: Don't interrupt. Two: I don't think I can cope with seeing you, Ricky, lolloping around the house like a bear with a sore head for much longer. Yes, I know we could send you out to join yet another sports club, but frankly I do enough ferrying you around. I look forward to those moments when you are comatose in front of the TV.

DAD: But surely …

MUM: I warned you.

DAD: Right. Yes.

MUM: Three: you (*to DAD*) are the worst.

DAD: Me? What have I done?

MUM: You're a hypocrite.

DAD: What?

MUM: Yes. A hypocrite. Don't pretend you don't know what I'm talking about. What were you looking at when I came into the kitchen suddenly yesterday?

DAD: The paper.

MUM: Wrong. The TV guide.

RICKY: Dad!

DAD: I was just …

MUM: Yes?

DAD: Err, you know, checking out the enemy.

JULIE: Right!

MUM: I saw you hurriedly close it. But not before I saw what you were looking at. The time for next week's live England match on TV. You'd always intended to get the telly back. But just one. For yourself – in the garage.

DAD: I …

MUM: No good covering up. I know there's an extension to the aerial in there.

DAD: Err. Right.

MUM: So … this time *I* make the rules.

Scene 7

Ricky's Bedroom.

RICKY *(on mobile)*:

Yeah, it's cool. Back to normal. Mum sorted Dad out. Yeah, we got the tellies back. But we have two telly-free nights a week. It's all right actually. I mean, if we miss something, we tape it, but actually we can't be bothered most of the time. Now it's radio, MP3s, the net, using the old moby … I mean, I dunno why Dad was hung up on TV, there's all this other stuff to worry about. I mean, there's this well wicked site I found. I'll text you the address. Problem is, Dad dominates the computer. We can never get on, but I'm gonna have to work on it, tell Dad I need it for my school work! They always fall for that one! Right, yeah, see you tomorrow at school, mate. And don't forget to ask me about that website. It is *totally* hot.

Happy 24

Characters

MILES: Miles Better, newsreader, mid-40s

CARETAKER: man in late 50s, early 60s

Scene 1

Newsdesk with stereotypical newsreader behind it.

Map of world, or image of Parliament behind him.

MILES: And here are the news headlines from Happy 24 – your 24-Hour Happy News Channel:

World Peace declared by all nations.

England win World Cup beating Germany 12–0 in final with four hat tricks by 17-year-old wonder-kid Michael Peckham.

Government promises free TVs, DVDs and laptops to all children over ten.

Everybody in the whole country to get a week's extra holiday.

No traffic jams reported during Bank Holiday.

All trains run on time.

Mrs McGinlay's cat Fluffy discovered alive and well and living in Norway.

And finally, education:

School uniform abolished.

Homework found to be unhealthy and banned in all schools.

School lunches to be replaced by McDonald's and food from that tasty Indian takeaway in Newland Street.

First, then, let's go to our main news story … I'm sorry, late news coming in …

God has been discovered living in a caravan in Norfolk. He tells reporters: 'It's all right. Heaven's a great place and everyone will be happy there, especially as we have lovely views and a fantastic Jacuzzi.'

And finally, some other breaking news …

Happy 24 News is to be taken off air. This will be the last ever Happy News broadcast. Research has shown that everyone is so contented they are not bothering to watch. In fact, there's not even any point in telling you more about the headlines because you're not watching, so, this is me, Miles Better, saying 'Goodnight' for the last time to our two remaining loyal viewers: my mum and my dog. Goodnight!

He taps a few buttons on the laptop, and then loosens his tie, and comes out from behind the desk. Looks around. Everyone has gone. Just a few studio lights still on.

MILES: Hello? Where is everyone?

A man shuffles forward. It is the CARETAKER. He is a dowdy, gloomy-looking character who is sweeping the floor with little or no enthusiasm.

CARETAKER *(glumly)*:
They've gone.

MILES: I know. Isn't it great?

CARETAKER: Is it?

MILES *(cheerily)*: Off to some party to celebrate Happy News finally reaching its goal.

CARETAKER: Its goal?

MILES: Of being obsolete. Everything's so wonderful there's only good news to report.

CARETAKER: Good news? They all lost their jobs. And you did too.

MILES: Yes … but who cares? Everything is so perfect, something or someone will come along and provide.

CARETAKER: I wouldn't bet on it. Life has a way of kicking you in the teeth.

MILES: But you heard: world peace declared!

CARETAKER: So what? Never had any problem in Silverwood Avenue. We're very peaceful. Though there was that time Mrs White let her hedge grow too high. A bit of fuss then … but that was sorted.

MILES: See? Everything comes up roses in the end.

CARETAKER: She didn't have roses.

MILES: No, I mean, there was a peaceful solution.

CARETAKER: Oh yes. She died.

MILES: That was the solution?

CARETAKER: No, someone bought her house. Didn't like hedges, so cut them down. That was the solution.

MILES: Oh. But what about the World Cup? Fantastic, isn't it?

CARETAKER: Don't like football.

MILES *(incredulously)*:
Everyone likes football. Michael Peckham's a hero.

CARETAKER: He's not mine. Not a patch on Alf Wigley.

MILES: Who does he play for?

CARETAKER: Don't play anything. He was my first boss. When I was Under Caretaker at Jenkinson's Biscuit Factory. He was a truly great caretaker. The way he handled a broom. Superb.

MILES: But what about traffic jams? No more of those.

CARETAKER: I like traffic jams. Makes the cars go slower.

MILES: What about the trains running on time? You must be pleased about that.

CARETAKER: Not particularly. I keep on missing them.

MILES: What?

CARETAKER: You see, I'm always late for things. Always have been. I was late for my wedding. My wife got fed up waiting and married the best man. Didn't see you reporting that.

MILES: When was it?

CARETAKER: Thirty-eight years ago.

MILES: Hardly news.

CARETAKER: It is to me. It still hurts. Still, it saved me a lifetime of arguments and rows. Anyway, point is, I'm always late, so I rely on the trains being late. That way I catch them.

MILES *(uncertainly)*:
I see … (*more brightly*) But what about God, eh? Can't say that's bad news, finding that he's living in Norfolk. Now we know heaven exists, what is there to worry about? I mean … Jacuzzis for everyone.

CARETAKER: Don't like Jacuzzis. Don't like any Japanese snacks.

MILES: It's not food.

CARETAKER: I agree. More like rubber.

MILES: No, what I mean is …

CARETAKER *(interrupting)*:
What I need is a bit of bad news to cheer me up.

MILES: Sorry?

CARETAKER: Bad news. Earthquake. Major company going bankrupt – that sort of thing. Makes me feel my own miserable, lonely and dull life isn't quite so bleak.

MILES: Tell you what. I've got an idea!

CARETAKER: Hope it's a bad one.

MILES: Absolutely dreadful. It'll definitely cheer you up.

CARETAKER: Not more good news. I can't stand it.

MILES: Wait there a moment.

CARETAKER: Not going anywhere. I missed my bus.

MILES races behind desk, presses a few buttons. A picture of a burning tank appears behind him.

MILES: The headlines today …

CARETAKER looks up with mild interest.

MILES: Superpowers at war: nuclear missiles heading for all major cities. World likely to end before supper.

Football: Germany come back in last five minutes to draw with England 12–12. Germans win World Cup on penalties after Michael Peckham slips on pair of knickers thrown by a female fan and misses penalty.

Train from Glasgow so late that male passengers all grow beards during journey.

Traffic jams on M25 so bad that drivers at back of queue get married, have children and retire before cars start moving again.

And finally … late news just in: the man from Norfolk who claimed he was God turns out to be Mr Frank Lee Lying, a man with a white beard who thought it'd be a laugh, and a good way of getting rid of those dodgy Jacuzzis he'd bought.

CARETAKER *(beaming)*:
Wonderful! Thank you, thank you. You've made a smelly and rather boring old man very happy.

MILES *(stands up and bows)*:
My pleasure, err, or should that be displeasure?

Blackout.

Island retreat

Characters

TAMSIN: pop-singer, mid-to late 20s

DAVID: her manager

FRED: press photographer for a tabloid newspaper

DIGGER: also press photographer for a tabloid newspaper

LIBBY: journalist with a tabloid newspaper

Scene 1

A tropical island.

The terrace of a single-storey beach house, on the edge of a small cliff, overlooking a bay of white sand. There are tropical plants on the terrace and a low fence surrounding it. From the terrace, there are views across the bay to other parts of the island. DAVID is on the terrace, standing by the garden table, cleaning his designer sunglasses. TAMSIN is on a sun-lounger, relaxing.

TAMSIN: Thank you for bringing me here. It's perfect.

DAVID: You know it's a private island, don't you?

TAMSIN: Private?

DAVID: It's owned by Philip Van Haden, that Dutch billionaire.

TAMSIN: So?

DAVID: Well, before I started managing you, I worked for Van Haden. He's let us have the beach house as a favour.

TAMSIN *(stretching)*: I need a break. We both do.

DAVID *(comes over to TAMSIN and kisses her)*: You deserve it. It's been a hard year. Can I get you a drink?

TAMSIN: Yes. Anything with ice in it.

DAVID: Wine? Gin?

TAMSIN: No, just sparkling water.

DAVID: I'm sorry, darling, I forgot.

TAMSIN: No problem. It's just, if I can kick it on holiday, then I can kick it anywhere.

DAVID: Of course, water and water coming up! (*disappears into the house*)

TAMSIN *(calls)*:
Do you think it's OK?

DAVID *(from inside)*:
The house?

TAMSIN: No, I mean … are we alone?

DAVID *(re-emerging)*:
I think so. There's another beach house, but you can only just see it. Look.

TAMSIN *(standing up)*:
I can't see it.

DAVID: There. Just above that strip of sand.

TAMSIN *(goes over to the fence and looks across the bay)*:
That's our nearest neighbour?

DAVID: Our only neighbour. I think it's Van Haden's son's place. Apparently he's never there.

TAMSIN: Great. Well, in that case, I'm going to work on that all-over tan. (*moves back towards the sun-lounger and takes the glass offered her by DAVID*)

DAVID: Are you sure?

TAMSIN: Do you object?

DAVID: Of course not, darling. I guess no one can see us.

TAMSIN: For once, the press are nowhere to be seen. And I'm free! (*downs the drink in one draught and then strides over the terrace back to the fence. Calls to the sea below*) Did you hear? You can't get me! I'M FREE!

Scene 2

Another part of the island.

Two men in their late 40s: FRED and DIGGER. FRED has a large camera on a tripod. DIGGER is holding his camera in his hands.

DIGGER: D'you get that, Fred?

FRED: Yep. Smack in the middle of my zoom. A real beauty.

DIGGER: Think how long we've been waiting.

FRED: Ooh. Five minutes?

DIGGER: Less. Three. Fantastic.

FRED: Didn't know you liked bird-watching.

DIGGER: Well, makes a change, don't it?

FRED: Yeah.

DIGGER: The Asian Cross-Billed Parrot. Distinctive because of its yellow and red striped bill. Hence the name.

FRED: Lovely. Add that to the collection when we get back. (*sighs*) What's her ladyship up to?

DIGGER: Oh, her? Nothing. So far she's had a drink.

FRED: Drink, eh? What?

DIGGER: Looked like water.

FRED: Could be vodka.

DIGGER: She's on the wagon.

FRED: So? She might have a quick drink when no one's looking.

DIGGER: Doubt it. Didn't you read all that stuff? About the doc saying she'd lose her voice if she kept on?

FRED: Read it? I took that photo of her leaving the surgery in those dark glasses. So, what else has she done?

DIGGER: From what I can see, not a lot. She's on holiday. What d'you expect?

FRED: We got to get something.

DIGGER: Patience, mate. Patience. We got all the time in the world. Besides, I want to get some more shots of Mr Cross-Billed Parrot. (*looks through lens*)

DIGGER: Bleeding Nora!

FRED *(stands up and grabs camera)*: What is it?

DIGGER: Look!

FRED: She's taking her …

DIGGER: I know! Why d'you think I called you? Cut the commentary! Get snapping!

FRED: What about your parrot?

DIGGER: Bugger the parrot. This is the bird I really wanna catch!

Scene 3

A flat in London.

TAMSIN is on the sofa, head in hands, crying. DAVID is next to her, his arm round her shoulder. On the floor and sofa, various newspapers are spread out, headlines blaring.

TAMSIN *(leans forward and picks a paper up at random)*: Look at this! (*stabs her finger at a headline and picture*) 'Topless Tammy bares all on island retreat.' (*tosses it to one side, picks up another*) 'Topless chart-topper pops out for a tan.' (*throws that aside too, and picks up a third*) And listen to this one. This is the worst of the lot: 'Teetotal Tammy on topless binge.' Binge? It was a glass of water! (*breaks away from DAVID, and goes to the drinks cabinet*)

DAVID: No! Don't, Tammy!

TAMSIN: Why should I listen to you? If I hadn't gone to that island, none of this would have happened!

DAVID *(attempts a joke)*: At least you're in the headlines.

TAMSIN *(gives him a withering look)*: What?

DAVID: Well – you said you needed more publicity.

TAMSIN: Yes! From my record company. For my music. Not this! I mean, that's why I hired you. To promote me. And my songs!

DAVID's mobile rings.

DAVID: Sorry. I'd better get this. (*moves towards side of room. Whispering*) Hi. Yeah, it's me. Twenty-five thousand. Half up front. If you're not interested, forget it. I've had other offers. I don't care if you're a quality paper, you still have to pay. (*snaps mobile lid shut*)

TAMSIN: Who was it?

DAVID: Some sleazy paper wanting an interview. I told them where to go.

TAMSIN: Thanks. Well, that's it. I'm finished. The public now think I'm a slut. Topless, with a married man …

DAVID: The divorce will be through next week.

TAMSIN: You said that last month.

DAVID: Bitch wouldn't sign the papers. I'm only married in name.

TAMSIN: Whatever. Who's gonna care about the truth? As far as everyone's concerned, I'm a tart. And they think I'm weak, too. Back on the booze. And I've been really strong. Haven't touched the stuff for ages. What I want to know is, how did those scum know I was on the island? And how did they get access to the beach house?

DAVID: Someone must have tipped them off. The airline. Security maybe. Did you tell anyone at the record company?

TAMSIN: No one. It was our little secret, remember?

DAVID: I'm sorry, darling. I really am.

Scene 4

The same flat.

Later. Buzz on the intercom.

DAVID: I'll get it. (*moves to intercom and picks it up*) Yes. You can come up. But tread carefully. She's a bit tender, if you know what I mean … and remember, not a word about you know what.

TAMSIN: Who is it?

DAVID: Oh, a friend. Nothing to worry about. By the way, darling, have you seen my sunglasses? They cost a hundred quid.

TAMSIN: Your sunglasses? Don't you think I've got other things on my mind?

DAVID: Err, yes. Sorry. But they do look rather good, so if you see them …

TAMSIN glares at him. Doorbell rings.

TAMSIN: David. Door.

DAVID answers it. There's DIGGER and a woman journalist, LIBBY.

TAMSIN: Who is it? (*stops in her tracks. To DAVID*) What are they doing here?

DAVID: I thought it'd be good if the papers heard your side of it.

TAMSIN: My side?

DAVID: Yes. Your version.

TAMSIN: My 'version'? There is no version. There is no 'my side'. There is no story! I had a holiday. I took my top off. I got a bit of a tan. I went home. That's it!

DAVID *(to the two visitors)*:
As you can see, she's a bit agitated.

TAMSIN: Don't talk about me as if I'm not here!

DAVID: I'm sure she'll calm down in a minute.

TAMSIN: Calm down? You invite the gutter press into my flat …

LIBBY: Gutter press?

DAVID: She doesn't mean it. I told you, she's a bit hysterical …

LIBBY: I thought you said she was ready, Dave.

TAMSIN: Dave? Dave? Do you two know each other?

DAVID: Err. Yes. Kind of.

TAMSIN: How 'kind of'?

DAVID: We go back a long way. Err … old …

TAMSIN: Old what?

LIBBY: He's my husband.

DAVID *(hissing)*:
I told you to keep quiet about that.

TAMSIN: Great. So, your ex-wife …

LIBBY: Ex?

TAMSIN: Well, soon-to-be divorced …

LIBBY: Divorced? What's she on about, Dave?

DAVID *(flustered)*:
Just a little joke. Anyway, I'm sure we can sort all this out after the interview.

TAMSIN: I'm not doing any interview.

DIGGER: You mean …

TAMSIN: And you can shut up too! (*suddenly realises who DIGGER is*) Wait a minute. You were on that boat on the way to the island. So, it's your pictures … (*picks up the newspaper and rolls it into a thick, tight tube*) Now, Mr …

DIGGER: Digger. Everyone calls me Digger. (*not realising the trouble he's in*) See, my name's Dennis Mole, or it could be 'digging the dirt', or perhaps …

TAMSIN *(interrupting, falsely polite)*:
Mr Mole, can I ask you a question?

DIGGER: Course. You don't want copies of those topless photos, do you? 'Cos they're quite tasteful, really.

TAMSIN *(advancing in a threatening manner)*:
Have you ever, by any chance, had a newspaper shoved up your …?

DIGGER *(suddenly aware of danger)*:
Err. Hang on, lady … don't do anything you'll regret …

TAMSIN *(getting closer)*:
Oh, I won't regret it.

DIGGER: Steady on, lass.

DIGGER backs out of room, followed by TAMSIN. LIBBY and DAVID wince as various sounds, 'Ow! Aaargh!', come from the hallway.

TAMSIN *(comes back in, minus newspaper)*:
He'll have difficulty reading *that* front page.

LIBBY: Right, I'm off. (*to DAVID*) I'll see you later. For supper?

TAMSIN *(bitterly)*:
Yes, you'd better go. Collect some toads, frogs and bats for the pot.

LIBBY *(ignoring her)*:
Coming? (*exits*)

TAMSIN (*to DAVID*):
Go on, you two-faced, greedy, slimy toe-rag.

DAVID: Look, I can explain.

TAMSIN: I bet you can.

DAVID: Are you going to be OK?

TAMSIN: Funnily enough, I feel just fine.

DAVID: Fine? You look … sort of …

TAMSIN: Angry? Vengeful? Murderous?

DAVID: Err, yes. I s'pose so.

TAMSIN: Well, David, darling, anger can be put to good use. You know what they say?

DAVID: Do I?

TAMSIN: Don't get angry, get even. And I've got two things to do to get even with you and that witch.

DAVID: Look, err … I'm going … like you wanted me to. (*starts backing out of the room*)

TAMSIN *(oblivious)*:
Firstly, I'm going to phone a reporter I know. I'm sure he'd love to hear how I was set up by my manager and his wife … or is it his ex-wife? Then, I'm going to write a song. A new sort of song. Not the lovey-dovey type. More like a punk record. Nu-metal even. Angry. Violent. Really rocking. And you know something, David?

DAVID *(by door, thinking he'd managed to get away)*:
What's that?

TAMSIN: So that everyone knows how you helped me, I'm gonna dedicate it to you. Oh, and finally …

DAVID: Yes?

TAMSIN: I think you forgot something. I found them under the *News of the World*. *(brings out DAVID's sunglasses and slowly crushes them in her hand, the metal snapping and twisting)* Here they are. *(hands them in a crumpled heap to him)*. A souvenir of our little holiday.

Gotta have faith

Characters

DAZ
JERMAINE
TREY
SONIA
SINDY
— all members of a band, Essential Crew

TREVOR: Trevor Horton, senior executive, DubGold Records

ALVIN: Alvin Knight, fashion/glamour photographer

Three ASSISTANTS: at photo shoot (non-speaking parts)

Scene 1

Warehouse.

Some crates, a couple of enormous speakers, a record deck, a guitar and a keyboard. DAZ is fiddling with some wires. TREY and SONIA are practising a dance routine.

TREY *(sings)*: If you ain't got faith
You ain't got me.

SONIA *(sings)*:
And if you ain't got faith
You can't be free.

TREY and SONIA try another dance move. It doesn't quite come off. They dissolve into laughter.

In struts JERMAINE, with SINDY.

JERMAINE: Hey, everyone.

DAZ *(looks up)*:
Hi, guys!

SINDY: Hiya, Daz.

SINDY and SONIA embrace.

TREY *(comes over and high fives JERMAINE)*:
What's up, bro?

JERMAINE: Listen up, y'all.

DAZ stands up, then sits on the edge of the speaker.

JERMAINE: We got it!

The others look unmoved. They have no idea what he's talking about.

SINDY: What Mr Smooth means is that the Essential Crew have got a studio session with … wait for it … DubGold Records.

TREY: No way, man. DubGold? They got all the top acts!

JERMAINE: And now they got us.

DAZ: That's cool. But ain't they into all that Gangsta Rap stuff?

SINDY: Yeah, but they do other stuff too. Besides, they're cool guys. And they're cool about all the faith stuff too.

JERMAINE: Besides, we don't wanna come across like no bible-bashing Christian band.

TREY: Why not? We're Christians. Ain't nothing to be ashamed of.

JERMAINE: I know, Trey. But we gotta get a foot in the door. We get too heavy now, we'll never get a record deal.

SINDY: You're awful quiet, Sonia. What's on your mind, girl?

SONIA: I don't know. Trey might be right. DubGold have some pretty heavy stuff. We always said we weren't gonna go for that crap. Guns. Dirty stuff. It's not our scene.

JERMAINE: No, it's not our scene. And they know that at DubGold. It's what makes us different. So, we should go for it, right?

DAZ: Definitely, man. Count me in.

JERMAINE: Sindy?

SINDY: I'm there.

JERMAINE: What 'bout you, Trey?

TREY: I don't know.

JERMAINE: It's the only offer we got. There are thousands of bands out there. What's gonna make Essential Crew get a deal when they don't?

SONIA: Stickin' to our principles.

JERMAINE: Right on, girl. DubGold ain't gonna make us do anything we don't wanna do. OK?

TREY: OK. I'm in.

SONIA: All right. But they start messin' with us, I'm walkin'.

JERMAINE *(stands up)*: Well, guys. We're on our way! Today north London. Tomorrow …

DAZ: South London …!

They all laugh.

JERMAINE: C'mon. Let's make some music!

Scene 2

Record company office.

Essential Crew lounging on white sofa. Behind the large desk is TREVOR Horton, of DubGold.

TREVOR: So, everything's cool, right?

JERMAINE: Yeah. That's one great studio.

TREVOR: Used by all the top bands and DJs.

SINDY: So, we got ourselves a deal?

TREVOR: We'll do a single. That's all. Like a promo track. Set you up for some interviews. Radio One. *Smash Hits. The Voice.* Get you on some kids' TV shows.

TREY: Sounds good, man.

TREVOR: And we'll want you to do some photo stuff. Moody shots. For the CD and for the press releases. OK?

SINDY: No problem. When d'you want us?

TREVOR: A car will pick you up on Friday from the studio, after you finish recording. In the meantime I'll speak to the press office and get them to set up a photo shoot. (*gets up, points the finger of an imaginary gun at them, and pulls an imaginary trigger*) You guys are gonna make a bang, I promise you. (*opens the door*)

The band stand up and troop out.

Scene 3

A dark, rather dingy street. Some bins against a wall covered in graffiti. It is, in fact, a set at a photo studio.

ALVIN and one of the ASSISTANTS are setting up large, angled standing lamps. Another ASSISTANT is sitting at a table, with a mirror on it, fiddling with make-up. Another ASSISTANT is by a stand with a variety of clothes hanging from it.

The band walk into the studio.

JERMAINE: Hey! This is cool.

ALVIN Knight, the photographer, walks towards them.

SINDY *(impressed)*:
You're Alvin Knight!

ALVIN: Hey! Who's this foxy lady?

SINDY *(blushing, holds out her hand)*:
My name's Sindy.

ALVIN *(laughs)*:
Sin by name, sin by nature?

SINDY *(giggles)*:
No, I'm a good, old-fashioned, church-going girl!

ALVIN: Glad to hear it. When we getting married?

They both laugh.

DAZ *(breaking in)*:
You did that cover that got banned, didn't you?

ALVIN: I might have.

DAZ: What was it called?

ALVIN: 'Comin' at you, babe.'

SINDY: '… the best of Black Street Music.'

JERMAINE: That's a well cool cover.

ALVIN: You got it?

JERMAINE: Err … no. I …

SONIA *(coolly, unimpressed by ALVIN)*:
What he's trying to say is we made a pact.

JERMAINE: Sonia!

SONIA: Not to buy music that supported gun culture or treated women like dirt.

ALVIN *(defensive)*:
Hey, ain't you comin' on a bit strong? That CD was a first class collection of cool tunes.

SONIA: It was a first class collection of all that's wrong with black music.

ALVIN *(to JERMAINE)*:
You sure you wanna do this? Your friend don't seem too keen.

JERMAINE: Sure? Sure? I been waitin' for this moment all my life, man!

ALVIN: Well, let's do it. Right, if you could get yourselves over by that wall.

SONIA *(to TREY)*:
This don't feel right.

TREY: Hey. The man's an artist. Give him a chance.

ALVIN: I want you to look mean and moody. You, Jermaine, at the front. Put your hands together and hold them in front of you, pointing at the camera, like this. (*takes up a pose as if he's holding two guns outstretched in front of him*)

JERMAINE: Like this?

ALVIN: You got it. (*turns to his ASSISTANT*) The bins.

The ASSISTANT goes over and tips over the bins. Rubbish falls out and spills on to the street.

ALVIN: Right, girls. I want you to hug right up to Daz and Trey. Like they're the most desirable guys in town.

SINDY *(laughs)*:
That'll take some real acting! (*sidles up to Daz and leans against him seductively*)

SONIA goes up to TREY and puts her hand limply on his shoulder.

ALVIN: Come on, girl! Put a bit of soul into it! I want 'sexy', I want 'hot' ... *(turns away again, and calls to the other ASSISTANT)* Can you put some make-up on her? And do something about those clothes.

SONIA: My clothes? What's wrong with them?

ALVIN: You look like a nun, babe. This ain't no bible convention. This is hot music!

SONIA: That's it. (*walking away*)

TREY: What's goin' on?

SONIA: I'm outa here. (*starts putting her jacket on*)

ALVIN: What's the matter?

SINDY: What's up, babe?

SONIA: You too blind to see? Too blind to notice what's happening here? I thought we was gonna be different. Not go down that route. I mean, is that what you want people to think? That black people exist only on the streets …

JERMAINE: Wait a minute, girl …

SONIA: No, you wait a minute, Jermaine. You listen to me. Look around you. A dark street? Trash cans? You pointing a gun?

JERMAINE: There ain't no gun. It's just a pose.

SONIA: Not this time. But what about when we sign that record deal? Then what's the excuse? It's our culture?

ALVIN: Hey, cool it! Don't take things so serious. This is just like dressing up when you were kids. Didn't you never do that? Kids who buy your music, it ain't serious. You think pop music ever changed anything? Think it ever stopped a war?

SONIA: That ain't the point. It's not about that. It's what I'm sayin' about myself. The kids who listen might not care less, but I care. That's what matters.

ALVIN: It's your call, girl. But what about the rest of the crew? What do they want? You gonna let them down?

JERMAINE *(to SONIA)*: If I don't do this, what have I got? I didn't do so well at school, 'case you forgot. I ain't no brain-box like you.

DAZ: I know where you're comin' from, Sonia. But I gotta stick with Jermaine. I dreamed of this all my life.

SONIA: Maybe you need to get better dreams, Daz.

TREY is sitting to one side, looking awkward.

SONIA: What about you, Trey? You gonna do this?

TREY: I'm sorry, sis. It's just pop music. I didn't do this for no politics or nothing.

SONIA: It ain't politics! We started at church. Don't that mean anything? You forgotten who gave us these voices?

TREY *(head down, almost apologetic)*: I only went to church 'cos I liked the singing.

SONIA looks at them, then at ALVIN.

ALVIN: Leave me outa this. This ain't my fight.

SONIA: If I leave here now, I ain't comin' back. Is that what you want?

No one says anything.

SONIA: I mean it.

TREY looks away. JERMAINE gets out his mobile and turns it over in his hands to avoid saying anything. DAZ keeps still, and quiet. SINDY says nothing.

SONIA starts to walk away. Suddenly SINDY stands up.

SINDY: Hey, Sonia, wait up!

JERMAINE: Where you goin'?

SINDY: What's it got to do with you? I'm just takin' a little walk with my friend.

JERMAINE: We … I … need you. I can't do them harmonies without you.

SINDY: There ain't no harmony if Sonia ain't in the group.

DAZ: Sindy!

SINDY: No point, Daz. I'm with Sonia. Good luck, guys. We'll see you around.

SINDY links arms with SONIA and the two of them disappear.

TREY: That's it then. I can just see the headline: 'The Essential Crew split after just one single'.

ALVIN starts packing camera away.

JERMAINE: Hey. Wait a moment.

ALVIN: I was told the whole package. Not just three guys looking depressed.

JERMAINE: So, we're finished. That'll be great for my street cred.

DAZ: There's only one thing for it. (*stands back smugly*)

TREY: What?

JERMAINE: Yeah. Spit it out!

DAZ: We'll have to form a boy band.

JERMAINE and TREY look at him like he's developed the plague. They start walking off.

DAZ: Hey, wait! It was just an idea, guys.

JERMAINE and TREY continue walking.

DAZ *(starting to walk after them)*:

Do you think the girls'd be open to bribery? 'Cos I could give 'em my collection of Beanies. Or what about some new members … like my sister … I mean, I know she's only seven but she's got a wicked voice … or there's my mum – she's no J-Lo, more like bungalow, her voice is so flat – but she's a cool dancer …

Fade as the three walk off.

Sherry darling

Characters

ZACH: Zach Turner, advertising copywriter

LOUISE: Louise Parkinson, advertising copywriter

ROSHEEN: their boss

MR HAWKSEY: owner of Hawksey Drinks Ltd

EXECUTIVES: several men and women (non-speaking parts)

ASSISTANT: Mr Hawksey's assistant

ELDERLY LADY: character in TV advert

Scene 1

A small, modern office.

Trendy dark glass on windows. A modernist print on the wall. One round table with two chairs. ZACH and LOUISE sit at a table. It has a single bottle of sherry in the middle.

ZACH: Doesn't matter how long we look at it.

LOUISE: Don't talk. Think.

ZACH: I am.

LOUISE: What can you see?

ZACH: Not a lot. Fuzzy black stuff. Then that stupid song by that boy band keeps on going through my mind.

LOUISE: Which one?

ZACH: Oh, I don't know. I don't even like it! Point is, I can't be very creative.

LOUISE: We have to! This is our last chance.

ZACH: It's sherry. Not a sports drink. Not vodka. Hardly trendy.

LOUISE: You know the score. This is our biggest client. If we lose the Hawksey portfolio we'll probably lose our jobs.

ZACH: But why us? Why do Hawksey want us to come up with a new campaign for their oldest brand? I mean, Hawksey's Sherry? Why not Peter and Annie? This is more their thing. We do trainers, we do energy bars, we do ...

LOUISE: … what they tell us to do. They want us to make Hawksey's Sherry hip and cool. They want us because we're hip and cool.

ZACH: I don't feel it. I mean, it's bloody sherry. My gran drinks it.

LOUISE: She's cool, your gran.

ZACH: Yeah, but she's not Madonna, is she?

LOUISE: I dunno – Madonna's getting on a bit. Point is, what we gonna do?

ZACH *(stands up and goes to window)*: Throw ourselves out?

Scene 2

Same office.

Much later. It is clearly evening. Light on in office. LOUISE leaning against wall, holding sherry glass, half-full. ZACH at table, laptop in front of him, sheets of paper with bright scribbles on table nearby. Sherry bottle still there.

LOUISE *(looking at sherry with distaste)*:
Disgusting.

ZACH *(exhausted)*:
What time is it?

LOUISE: Nine o'clock.

ZACH: Great.

LOUISE: What have we got?

ZACH: Here's the list so far: We show a red-faced tramp holding a bottle of Hawksey's. 'So disgusting it'll help you give up drinking' then we cut to him being sick in a dustbin.

LOUISE: That one's a joke, right?

ZACH: That's the best we have.

LOUISE: Seriously? Surely we can do better than that.

ZACH *(sighs)*:
OK. Trendy girls in bar. Cut to boys laughing at them 'cos they're drinking Hawksey's, then Martin Kemp comes in and goes over to girls. Boys clearly envious. Out on the girls leaving with Kemp. He winks at camera as he leaves. Close on bottle of Hawksey's on bar. 'Dare to be different' whispered by sexy female voice.

LOUISE: That's brilliant! We thought of that?

ZACH: We did. Unfortunately the only reason we thought of it was because it already exists.

LOUISE: It does?

ZACH: Don't you watch TV?

LOUISE: Not if I can help it. Can't stand all those ads.

ZACH: Well, you must have seen this one without noticing it. It's for port. Sedgeforth's Port.

LOUISE: It is?

ZACH: 'Fraid so. That's the sum total of four hours' work. A sick joke that would get us sacked in five seconds … and someone else's ad campaign.

LOUISE: Not just anyone's ad campaign.

ZACH: What d'you mean?

LOUISE: Sedgeforth's. They're Hawksey's greatest rivals.

ZACH: Even better.

LOUISE: Where's the newspaper?

ZACH: Why? Got an idea?

LOUISE: No. I need to look for a new job.

Scene 3

Boardroom.

Large, oval table with screen at one end. ZACH and LOUISE by the screen. Gathered around the table, several EXECUTIVES in business suits. Their boss, ROSHEEN, is standing. MR HAWKSEY and his ASSISTANT are sat next to one another.

ROSHEEN: Well, without further ado, I'll hand over to Zach Turner and Louise Parkinson, who, I'm sure need no introduction.

LOUISE and ZACH stand up.

LOUISE: Err. Thank you, Rosheen. Zach ...

ZACH: Right, yes. Fantastic. Good to see you Mr Hawksey. How's Mrs Hawksey?

MR HAWKSEY *(without smiling)*: Still divorced.

ZACH: Ha! Glad to see the old Hawksey sense of humour still going strong. Unlike the marriage! *(laughs at his own joke, peters out as he realises no one else is laughing)*

ROSHEEN: Cut to the chase, Zach. Mr Hawksey has another meeting at 11.

ZACH: Of course. Louise ... over to you. *(sits down abruptly)*

LOUISE *(glares at Zach)*:
Thank you, Zach. Well, as you know, we were tasked with …

MR HAWKSEY: Get on with it! How are you going to improve the sales of Hawksey's Sherry?

LOUISE: Well, we have an ad campaign to die for.

MR HAWKSEY: I'm listening.

LOUISE: The gist of it is built around this. Zach?

ZACH hits the button on the mouse of the laptop. A picture of Zach with three mates in a bar in Spain comes up on the screen. They are all drinking heavily from lager bottles. They have no clothes on. ZACH cannot see the screen.

MR HAWKSEY: Is this some kind of joke?

ZACH: Good, isn't it?

LOUISE *(notices image on screen and hisses)*:
Zach! Look! Your holiday pic!

ZACH *(stares, horrified at screen. Then tries to cover up)*:
Ah ha. Exactly the response I was expecting. Shock. Surprise. Leading me to … (*clicks mouse again*)

A new image comes up on screen: of Hawksey's Sherry, with a slogan: 'Dare to be different'.

MR HAWKSEY: I like it. Though it seems …

ZACH: A little familiar?

MR HAWKSEY: Yes.

ZACH: We're coming to that. Louise?

LOUISE: Right. Well, the ad campaign would basically show some guys in a bar. They are eyeing up three trendy, sexy-looking girls, but when they see them drinking Hawksey's Sherry, they turn away in disgust.

ZACH: Then, this well known, drop-dead gorgeous TV or film actor will come in – you know, like Martin Kemp – and he'll clock the three girls, go up to them, and they'll all go off arm in arm. The boys are left dumbfounded. It ends with Kemp – or whoever – winking at them over his shoulder as he leaves. Then, the slogan comes up. 'Dare to be different. Drink Hawksey's Sherry.'

ASSISTANT: Mr Hawksey …

MR HAWKSEY *(ignoring her)*: I like it. Brilliant.

ASSISTANT *(more urgently)*: Mr Hawksey!

MR HAWKSEY *(impatiently)*: What is it?

ASSISTANT whispers long and hard in his ear.

MR HAWKSEY *(with a face like thunder)*: What? I knew I'd seen that idea somewhere before!

ZACH: Exactly.

MR HAWKSEY: Sedgeforth's. Our biggest rival!

LOUISE: If we can explain …

MR HAWKSEY: That campaign has won awards.

ZACH: I know. Good, isn't it?

MR HAWKSEY: Yes, you fool. But it's not yours!

LOUISE: Ah ha! And that's what's clever about it.

MR HAWKSEY: And how is it clever?

ZACH: Well, when we do the campaign and launch it, it's inevitable that Sedgeforth's will be absolutely furious. They will almost certainly take you to court …

MR HAWKSEY: And that's good?

LOUISE: It's brilliant! You want Hawksey's Sherry to come across as mean and hip. Well, what better way than to steal someone else's idea. Everyone loves a villain. Imagine how surprised people will be. Hawksey's, they'll say, I didn't believe they had it in them.

ZACH: Then, just before the court case, you withdraw the ad. By that time you'll have made the front page of the papers, and everyone will be talking about it.

MR HAWKSEY: It could cost me hundreds of thousands.

LOUISE: Yes. But think how much ad campaigns cost. You can't buy this sort of publicity.

MR HAWKSEY is silent. He taps his pen on the desk. Then he stands abruptly, followed by his ASSISTANT. He marches to the door, then turns.

MR HAWKSEY: I'll be in touch.

MR HAWKSEY and his ASSISTANT leave. ZACH and LOUISE look at each other, then at ROSHEEN.

ZACH: Wanna see some more holiday photos?

Scene 4

Zach and Louise's office.

Laptop is perched on the desk, the back of the screen to the audience. ZACH and LOUISE are watching it.

LOUISE: Got the CD?

ZACH: Yeah. It's in there. Can't wait to see what it looks like.

LOUISE: Go on then.

ZACH clicks mouse.

The following can be acted out. It is the advert they are watching.

An ELDERLY LADY, well dressed, is sitting by a table. She is playing solitaire. A letter falls through the letter-box. She picks the letter up and reads it out loud.

ELDERLY LADY: 'We are delighted to inform you that you have won the Prize Crossword competition. Please find enclosed vouchers to the value of fifty pounds.' This calls for a celebration. (*moves back to table. There is a bottle of Sedgeforth's Port on it. Pushes it to one side*) A real celebration. (*opens the cupboard and removes a bottle of Hawsksey's Sherry. Pours a glass and lifts it to her lips*)

VOICE-OVER: Have a change. Have a Hawksey's.

Fade lights or exit ELDERLY LADY.

ZACH *(halts CD)*: That's it. That's the new ad. And Hawksey loves it. Well, our strategy worked.

LOUISE: Just. For a moment, I actually thought Hawksey was going to go with your original idea.

ZACH: So did I. Thank God he saw sense.

LOUISE: Decided he wasn't so keen on sexing-up sherry after all. I think we shocked him. Lucky he didn't take the business elsewhere.

ZACH: Mind you, I feel sorry for Peter and Annie having to write that stuff instead of us.

LOUISE: Don't. It'll probably win awards. And it saved our jobs.

ZACH: Fancy a drink?

LOUISE: Yeah, why not? What have we got?

ZACH *(opens drawer of table and pulls out sherry bottle):* Oops.

LOUISE: What? You finished it?

ZACH: It grows on you.

LOUISE: Hair grows on you. Doesn't mean I want to drink it!

ZACH: It's not that bad.

LOUISE: Well, I'm going for a proper drink. Coming?

ZACH: Yeah. OK. You know what I fancy?

LOUISE: What?

ZACH: Sedgeforth's Port. It's quite trendy nowadays. 'Dare to be different' is what we say.

LOUISE: Who says?

ZACH: Me and Martin Kemp.

LOUISE and ZACH exit.

The truth about Gina

Characters

PHIL: deputy head

SHEILA: headteacher

TONY, JAN, SAM — Year 11 pupils

STEVEN: Year 7 boy

DANIELS: Rod Daniels, reporter on local paper

BARBARA: Barbara Turner, editor of local paper

FIONA: receptionist

OLDER GIRL: aged 17–18

GINA'S MUM (or DAD)

Scene 1

Headteacher's office.

A man in a suit, PHIL, sits on a chair. A woman, SHEILA, the headteacher, stands looking out of the window. There is a phone on the desk. Suddenly, it rings. PHIL stands up.

SHEILA *(without turning round)*:
Don't answer it, Phil.

PHIL *(stops and sits down)*:
We have to answer it some time.

SHEILA: Yes. But not now. Not yet.

Fade lights.

Slowly, bring up lights on downstage left and set-up for scene 2.

Scene 2

In the school grounds.

Group of school friends (TONY, JAN and SAM), some sitting on, some standing round a bench. They seem in a similar mood to the two adults.

TONY: Can't believe it.

JAN: She weren't no angel.

SAM: What was she doing? I mean, going off like that.

TONY: Who knows?

JAN: She was always wild. Did her own thing.

TONY: Haven't you thought about it?

JAN: About what?

TONY: Why she did it.

JAN: Perhaps she didn't do it.

SAM: What's going to happen in school?

JAN: Who cares?

SAM: We'll get the blame from her mum and dad. It'll be us.

TONY: We had nothing to do with it.

JAN: He means the school. We're all in it. Like it or not.

Scene 3

Headteacher's office.

SHEILA is holding a letter in her hand. There is a knock on the door.

SHEILA: Come in.

A small boy, STEVEN pokes his head round the door.

SHEILA: Hello, Steven.

STEVEN *(comes in)*:
They're ready for you, miss. Mr Carpenter said to get you.

SHEILA: All of Year 11?

STEVEN: I think so, miss.

SHEILA: Thank you. Tell him I'll be along in a minute.

Lights down.

Scene 4

Assembly hall.

SHEILA at the front of the stage, facing out.

SHEILA: Good morning, Year 11. What I have to tell you is not easy. Some of you … most of you … will have heard the news this morning, but for those of you who haven't, what I have to say will come as a shock. (*removes her glasses, and holds them in her right hand by her side*)

Last night, at about 7 pm, the police called me to say they had found the body of Gina Baker at the foot of the flats on Carhill Estate. They believe she had been dead for only a short while but, of course, it is all speculation for the moment. As some of you may know, Gina left the school suddenly on Thursday afternoon, during last lesson. There is no reason to suspect that Gina's death was anything but an accident, or that her leaving was in any way connected to what happened, but I need to tell you now that the police will be coming to the school later today. They will want to speak to a number of you about Gina. (*pauses, and puts her glasses on again*)

I know this news is terribly hard to bear. Many of you will be Gina's friends or classmates. I also want you to know that if any of you feel too upset in class today, I have instructed your teachers to let you leave the classroom and come to the school office. Somebody will be there if you wish to talk.

Finally, I understand that this is a very short explanation of a tragic event. No doubt you have many questions you wish to ask me. I am not sure I am in a position to answer these now, but I will try to speak to you again later today or tomorrow.

One final point. It is inevitable that reporters from local television and newspapers will want to speak to you. I cannot stop you speaking to them. But I will say just this. Be careful what you do say. Think about what Gina would have wanted. Until we know the truth about what happened it's best not to say anything.

Good morning. *(exits)*

Lights down.

Scene 5

In the school grounds.

TONY and SAM are passing a basketball between them.

TONY: D'you speak to them, then?

SAM: Who?

TONY: Those reporters.

SAM: Nah. Anyway, they wouldn't want to know.

TONY: Know what?

SAM: That she was a cow.

TONY: What you talking about? She wasn't even in your form.

SAM: So? I saw her round school. She was in my ICT class. Well, when she turned up. Last time, she chucked some of Jan's Coke into the DVD drive.

TONY: Yeah, but …

SAM: Look, all I'm saying is what Jan said. She weren't no angel.

TONY: I know. Don't mean she deserved what happened to her.

SAM: I'm not saying that. I'm not saying anything. (*throws the ball hard at TONY and walks off*)

TONY: Oi. Wait up! (*follows SAM*)

Scene 6

Headteacher's office.

PHIL sinks into a chair. SHEILA is already sitting.

PHIL: What a day! Don't know how we got through it.

SHEILA: Thanks for your support. I thought the staff were excellent. Fewer kids in tears than I expected, too.

PHIL: You've spoken to Mr and Mrs Baker?

SHEILA: Yes. (*sighs*) We're already into the blame game. And I couldn't really defend us, could I? I mean, a girl runs off in the middle of the lesson, and no one notices. No one knows that a gang had jumped her at lunchtime. No one knows that all last week she had stayed out each evening until midnight on Carhill Estate, drinking with some group of girls who'd left school.

PHIL: Not even her parents knew?

SHEILA: So they say. But what parents wouldn't know?

PHIL: You mean you never sneaked out as a teenager?

The phone rings.

SHEILA: Not every night. In any case, my parents would have been on to me like a flash. I expected it.

The phone's still ringing.

PHIL: It could be anybody.

SHEILA: No. It'll be them. The press.

Scene 7

A bench by the school.

SAM and JAN are both sat looking at the front page of a paper. SAM throws the paper down on the bench.

SAM: Adults! Why can't they tell the truth? Just tell it like it is?

JAN: It's not all adults.

SAM: Yeah. Right.

JAN: No – look, what did you expect? (*reads from paper*) Gina was a popular and talented girl at Fairmount High. Friends and family have lined up to say how lovely she was. 'She was full of fun and laughter,' said her uncle, Philip Baker. 'She was always a practical joker, and her pranks had us all in stitches.'

SAM (*snorts*):
Practical joker? Tell that to that girl in Year 9 she beat up. And Miss Caffrey. She made her life hell. Not that I feel sorry for her, she was a crap teacher, but it's like suddenly Gina is Saint Gina Baker of Fairmount High.

JAN: Hear what they said about the school: 'Fairmount High has a long history of bullying, and of failing to deal with the consequences. Staff knew about Gina's unhappiness, but failed to deal with it, or the bullying she suffered.'

SAM: First part's right at least.

JAN: Come on. It's not that bad. Carpenter sorted out that stuff when we were in Year 7. You know – those Year 10s.

SAM: Maybe. But they still hide the truth. All schools do. Look at that leaflet they give out to new parents. 'Come to Fairmount High: winner of Achievement in Schools PE Excellence Award.'

JAN: So? We did win it.

SAM: But have you seen the picture they put on the leaflet? It was of the games pavilion. What they didn't show was the front, where the paint's all peeling off. I put my foot through one of the steps last week. And that crap today from the head. Why can't she tell us everything she knows? Perhaps the paper's right …

Man enters from left. He is Rod DANIELS, a reporter.

DANIELS: Hello. I'm Rod Daniels. I work for the *Fairmount Observer*.

SAM: Goodbye. (*starts to leave*)

DANIELS: Wait. Look … I just want to put the record straight.

SAM stops.

JAN: What do you mean?

DANIELS: Well – you go to Fairmount High, don't you?

SAM *(turning)*: So?

DANIELS: This Gina Baker business. Doesn't make sense to me.

SAM: Nor me.

JAN *(to SAM)*: Don't say anything.

DANIELS: Look, you've got it all wrong.

JAN: What do you want?

DANIELS: I'm not even on the Baker story. But even I read the front page – like you probably did. All that stuff about Gina being wonderful.

JAN: So, we read it. So what?

DANIELS: Wonderful? That's not what I heard.

SAM: Too right!

DANIELS: I heard she was a real bully, that she'd picked on lots of kids.

JAN: Maybe.

DANIELS: Then there was that incident on Thursday – or was it Wednesday …

DANIELS is fishing, but SAM and JAN don't realise.

SAM: How do you know about that?

DANIELS: It's my job. Anyway, lots of other kids at the school told me.

SAM: So, you know about her being beaten up on Thursday lunchtime. 'Bout that gang? They'd just had enough.

DANIELS: Yeah – just wanted to check it out with someone reliable. Like you two. (*to SAM*) Were you there?

SAM: Not exactly. I heard all about it from a mate though. Gina had picked on some little Year 7. Didn't realise she had a big sister.

DANIELS: What about you?

JAN: When I arrived it was all over. Everybody disappeared before the teachers came.

DANIELS: So, everyone had had enough of her?

SAM: Looks like it. Thing is, they weren't from the school …

SHEILA appears at side of stage. JAN and SAM don't see her.

DANIELS *(sees SHEILA, but he has his story)*: Look, you've been great. What are your names? I could send you some free cinema vouchers if you want.

JAN: Jan Davis. Look, don't you want to know about …

DANIELS *(interrupting)*: I think that's my pager. Probably some little old lady's cat got stuck up a tree. That'll be my story (*laughs*) …

SAM: Don't you want to know my name?

DANIELS: No – it doesn't matter. One's enough. I can send the tickets to your friend.

DANIELS exits. SHEILA comes across to JAN and SAM.

SHEILA: Come on, you two. How come you're still hanging around here?

JAN: Just chatting really.

SAM: Yeah. But we're off now.

SHEILA: And what did that man want?

JAN: Who, miss?

SHEILA: That reporter, Rod Daniels.

SAM: Nothing. Just wanted to chat.

SHEILA: Come on.

JAN: Honestly, he didn't want anything.

SHEILA: Did you know he was reporting on Gina's death?

JAN: He said he wasn't on that story.

SAM: Said he didn't like the front-page article.

SHEILA: And you believed him?

SAM: He seemed all right.

SHEILA: I'm sure he did.

JAN (*cross*): I knew it. Knew we should have kept our mouths shut.

SAM: Yeah. Seen and not heard. That's what my dad says about kids. I always thought he was joking.

SHEILA: You'd better both come back to school for ten minutes. Tell me what you did say.

Scene 8

Local paper office.

SAM bursts in. There's a woman, BARBARA, by a desk. SAM assumes she's a receptionist. She is flicking through a copy of the paper.

BARBARA: What is it?

SAM: I need to see Rod Daniels.

BARBARA: He's not here. Can I take a message?

SAM *(flings a copy of the paper down in front of her)*: Yes, you certainly can! You can tell him what we think of him. Me and Jan Davis. Yeah, get the spelling right. Davis with an 'i' not 'ie'. And Sam Parker. That's P A R K E R. (*spells it out*) But you can put down what you want. Whatever message you want. Because you always do, don't you?

BARBARA: Look, I think you'd better …

SAM: No, you listen to me. Gina weren't no angel, but we never saw anything at lunchtime on that day. It was just what we were told. And the kids who beat her up – if they beat her up – weren't even from our school. And my friend Jan – she can't even show her face in school because your front page has her on it, saying how the school did nothing about the fighting, how they didn't protect Gina – and how she got jumped by a gang of older girls. It was me who said that! Not Jan.

BARBARA: I think you'd better leave.

SAM: Don't worry. I'm going! Can't bear to stay a moment longer … *(starts to leave)*

BARBARA: Just one thing …

SAM *(stops)*: What?

BARBARA: Have you ever considered we might be right?

SAM: What are you talking about? Daniels made it up. We didn't know anything. Not really.

BARBARA: Perhaps some of it's wrong. Perhaps some of it's right.

SAM: And that's good enough?

BARBARA: Look. If we hit a few targets then perhaps it's worth it. Are you telling me the school's not got problems with bullying?

SAM: I'm not telling you anything. Not after Daniels … Anyway, who are you? I thought you were …

BARBARA: Just a receptionist?

SAM *(red-faced)*:
Aren't you?

BARBARA: No.

SAM: So, who are you?

BARBARA: I'm the editor. Barbara Turner. It's all about perception, isn't it?

SAM: I don't get it.

BARBARA: You assumed I was the receptionist. Like we assumed Gina was bullied. Based on evidence. Who knows? I might have been. How were you to know?

At that moment, another woman, FIONA comes into the reception area.

BARBARA: Ah, Fiona, you're back. This young man wants to make an appointment with Rod Daniels. Can you check the diary?

FIONA: Of course. What's your name?

SAM: No, it's OK. I've gotta go. (*exits*)

Scene 9

Headteacher's office.

SHEILA and PHIL standing.

SHEILA: I'll need to speak to Year 11 again. Put the record straight.

PHIL: I'll send a note round to the form teachers. You want to see them now?

SHEILA: No – at afternoon registration: 2 pm in the hall.

PHIL: What are you going to tell them?

SHEILA: The truth, what else?

PHIL: Is that wise?

SHEILA: Probably not. But it's about time they heard the facts.

PHIL: If we know the facts.

SHEILA: Well, I'll tell them what I believe to be the facts.

PHIL: The truth?

SHEILA: As close to it as possible.

Scene 10

Assembly hall.

SHEILA stands in front of school.

SHEILA: I'm sorry that it has taken a couple of days before I could speak to you all again. By now, many of you will have read the allegations in the paper, about how the school stood by and did nothing. About Gina's unhappiness. You will also know that members of your year group have been quoted in the article. There is no point hiding these matters. Well, I have spoken to the police, and I think it is only right I tell you the truth, as I understand it. And the truth about this school.

Lights fade.

Then lights up.

A horseshoe of figures: TONY, SAM, JAN, STEVEN, SHEILA, PHIL, an OLDER GIRL, BARBARA DANIELS, GINA'S MUM. The following lines are delivered to the audience, not to each other. It should build up speed until the end when SHEILA speaks.

TONY: She was all right. A laugh.

SAM: I heard she picked on kids.

STEVEN: She picked on me.

GINA'S MUM: We couldn't control her.

OLDER GIRL: She liked a drink.

TONY: She was a laugh.

SAM: She was a cow.

PHIL: I sorted out that problem she caused with Year 7.

DANIELS: I sorted out the facts.

OLDER GIRL: I sorted her out.

BARBARA: I sorted out the front page.

JAN: I didn't recognise myself.

SAM: I didn't recognise Gina.

DANIELS: She was pushed.

OLDER GIRL: She was drunk.

PHIL: She fell.

DANIELS: Pushed.

OLDER GIRL: Drunk.

PHIL: Fell.

OLDER GIRL: Drunk!

PHIL: Fell!

DANIELS: Pushed!

SHEILA *(steps forward from horseshoe)*: The truth is, Gina …

Instant blackout.

The first casualty

Characters

GENERAL: General Alexander Irons, in charge of local allied forces

MILWORTHY: Susannah Milworthy, spokesperson, allied forces

JAMES: James Midler, cameraman and reporter, late 30s

LAURA: Laura Taggart, reporter, her first conflict, late 20s

Scene 1

A briefing room at a military base.

GENERAL Alexander Irons and Susannah MILWORTHY are sat at a desk, with a map behind them. JAMES and LAURA are sat opposite them, among other reporters.

MILWORTHY: That brings us to the end of the briefing. General Irons has kindly agreed to answer two final questions. Can I remind you please to identify yourself as you ask each question?

JAMES: James Midler, Reuters. General Irons, can you give us an accurate update of the situation in Sirghiz? We have heard unconfirmed reports that there is open warfare on the streets.

GENERAL: Our boys entered the outskirts of the city last night and met only sporadic resistance. As liberators, they were broadly welcomed by the inhabitants, but those factions still loyal to President Sharif were neutralised as and when it was required.

LAURA: Laura Taggart, *The Times*. We have been told that there was widespread bombing of civilian areas by allied planes, with a hospital and school being hit. Is this true?

GENERAL: We have used smart bombs to target military bases. I cannot confirm these stories, but can only say that there is widespread evidence that the President's troops have used civilian locations to hide weapons of mass destruction, dirty bombs and so on. Clearly, the enemy is still active and remains a threat to our forces. They will use any means, fair or foul, to knock us off course.

JAMES: So, does that mean …

MILWORTHY: Thank you, ladies and gentlemen. That's the end of the briefing.

JAMES: Sorry, can I just clarify …

MILWORTHY and IRONS stand up.

JAMES *(calls out)*:
General, is Sirghiz under control?

MILWORTHY: No more questions.

LAURA: Are allied forces in trouble?

GENERAL *(turning as he leaves)*:
Let me make it clear. Sirghiz has been secured by our forces, and the situation is as we expected it to be at this stage. Things are progressing well.

JAMES: So, it's safe?

The GENERAL leaves, with MILWORTHY. LAURA and JAMES are left in room.

LAURA:	What do you reckon?
JAMES:	Who knows? They won't let you near Sirghiz unless you're with a patrol. Even then we end up stuck on the outskirts.
LAURA:	Is it worth a try?
JAMES:	Could be. Know a local driver?
LAURA:	Yeah. Can you bring your interpreter?
JAMES:	Sure – if he's up for it. He wasn't too keen when I talked to him earlier. But then he doesn't come from Sirghiz.
LAURA:	OK. Seven o'clock?
JAMES:	Fine. See you outside the hotel.

Scene 2

Sirghiz.

JAMES and LAURA crouching by a wall, the crackle of gunfire overhead.

JAMES: I thought this place was secure.

LAURA: So did I. Did you get any decent shots?

JAMES: A few, but it's too dangerous to get any closer.

LAURA: What happened to Mohammed?

JAMES: He's waiting at the jeep.

A sudden longer burst of gunfire.

JAMES: That was bloody close! Where was it from?

LAURA: Our lot, I think.

JAMES: The liberators.

LAURA: Liberators? The only thing they're going to liberate is my head from my body.

JAMES: Here, stick this on. (*hands LAURA a helmet*)

LAURA: I've already tried it. Doesn't fit. And I don't like the colour. Clashes with my top.

JAMES: Look, we need to get out of here.

LAURA: Why the hell didn't they tell us it was like this?

JAMES: Perhaps they didn't know.

LAURA: Yeah – and perhaps the President is a kind guy who loves animals and children.

JAMES: All right, I'll call Davie on the two-way, tell him to meet us by that burnt-out shop.

LAURA: Right, I'll go first … (*gets up to run, but there is a sudden burst of fire. She falls to the ground clutching her arm*)

LAURA: Bastard got me!

JAMES *(runs over)*:
You OK?

LAURA: Find the bullet.

JAMES: Don't be stupid. I'm not a doctor.

LAURA: I don't mean that! It went straight through. It's in the wall there. Christ it hurts!

JAMES: Here. (*pulls his top off, rips off some cloth and ties it round LAURA'S arm*)

LAURA: I'm OK. Get the bullet.

JAMES: No point. Didn't you read your history books? Even if it was one of them who shot you, we made the bullets. We've been supplying them with arms since the '87 war. It won't prove anything.

LAURA: All right, wise guy. Get me out of here. I've had enough of the sightseeing trip. It's over-rated, I prefer Paris in the spring.

JAMES: There's Davie. Come on. Keep your head down.

JAMES props LAURA up as they move towards the jeep.

Scene 3

Army hospital.

JAMES by LAURA's bed. She's sitting up, reading Hello! *magazine.*

JAMES: Hiya.

LAURA (*putting magazine down*):
Hi. Sorry, I'll put this down.

JAMES: No, you're all right. Got to do your research.

They both laugh.

JAMES: Besides, where'd you get that?

LAURA: I liberated it from Jenny's rucksack. It's two months old. Did you know Kat's got a new man in *EastEnders*?

JAMES: Kat? Who's Kat?

LAURA: You *have* been away a long time.

JAMES: Anyway. How are you?

LAURA: As I thought, the bullet went straight through. All that flesh. Just as well I didn't start the diet.

JAMES: So, how long they keeping you in?

LAURA: Just today. Long as I keep the dressing on, I should be OK. Then I'm going back.

JAMES: What – home?

LAURA: Are you kidding? No. Sirghiz.

JAMES: Me kidding? Are you sure that bullet didn't go straight through your brain, take a few cells out on the way?

LAURA: I mean it. Look. They said Sirghiz was secure.

JAMES: General Irons said that because we pushed him into saying it.

LAURA: Well, we know it isn't.

JAMES: Be fair. He also said the enemy was 'still active'.

LAURA: He also went on about them having been 'neutralised'. Didn't seem very neutralised when they were firing at us.

JAMES: So, file your story and move on.

LAURA: It's not enough. I think there's all sorts going on in the centre of Sirghiz.

JAMES: Wait until it's safe. Go in with soldiers around you.

LAURA: I know what you're saying, but I'm fed up with being embedded, controlled by what the army allow me to see, five miles and five days behind the action.

JAMES: There's no point in being a hero. Everyone says the same. Get your story, but don't take unnecessary risks.

LAURA: Was yesterday unnecessary?

JAMES: No, of course not. We got an exclusive, and showed people what was really happening.

LAURA: So – we do it again. But take even more precautions. We'll go in at night – wear local clothing.

JAMES: You've got it all worked out.

LAURA: It's the only way.

JAMES: Well, we've got to see Susannah Milworthy first.

LAURA: Have we?

JAMES: Yes. I got a message saying she needed to see us urgently.

LAURA: Things are looking up. Perhaps she's softening.

JAMES: I wouldn't bet on it.

Scene 4

Office at military base.

MILWORTHY sitting on edge of desk. LAURA and JAMES stood in room.

MILWORTHY:	Thanks for coming in.
JAMES:	No problem.
LAURA:	What is it?
MILWORTHY:	This is difficult.
LAURA:	I've heard those words before. Usually before some guy back home dumps me.
JAMES:	Come on, spit it out.
MILWORTHY:	All right. General Irons has instructed me that you are to be denied protective coverage during your reporting.
JAMES:	What does that mean in plain English?
MILWORTHY:	It means you've lost your protection. No more riding in a tank at the back of the queue.
JAMES:	Why?
MILWORTHY:	Officially, it's too much risk having you there – too much risk to you, and to the soldiers who have a job to do.

LAURA: And unofficially?

MILWORTHY: Off the record?

LAURA: OK.

MILWORTHY: You filed the wrong report. Saying Sirghiz was unsafe, that we didn't have control. It undermined the confidence of the troops. I mean, whose side are you on?

JAMES: It's a cliché, but we're on the side of truth.

MILWORTHY: Are you now? So, you and your producers would never edit out boring shots of soldiers standing peacefully guarding a school, when there's a five-minute food riot to show instead?

LAURA: That's a cheap shot.

MILWORTHY *(gesturing at James' camera)*: And so are many of yours. So, don't lecture me on truth.

JAMES: Come on, Laura, there's no point waiting here. We've got to find ourselves a driver and a jeep … get into Sirghiz.

JAMES and LAURA start to leave.

MILWORTHY: Oh, one thing.

LAURA: What is it? Got another half-fact to tell us?

MILWORTHY: No. This one's true. You can check it on TV tonight. If you'd been more careful you might even have been there to report it.

LAURA: Report what?

MILWORTHY: Allied forces took control of Sirghiz in the early hours of the morning. The city centre is entirely secure. General Irons himself is appearing in the next ten minutes on live television outside the President's palace. I think CNN have the exclusive for that one. Shame you missed it. Personally, I wouldn't bother with Sirghiz. It's yesterday's news. (*turns and leaves by another exit*)

LAURA: Bitch!

JAMES: She's only doing her job.

LAURA: Still, she had to rub it in.

JAMES: You know something? She used to work for the BBC. A top reporter. Before your time. Then she got wounded in Kosovo. Apparently she was very lucky. The bullet went straight through her.

LAURA *(sitting on the edge of the table, gingerly rubbing her injured arm)*:

I never believed it before.

JAMES: What?

LAURA: You know. That saying.

JAMES: What saying?

LAURA: The first casualty of war is truth.

JAMES: Oh, that old one. Well, it sounds good.

LAURA: It sounds good because it's true.

JAMES *(more brightly)*:
Come on, I think I know a man we should speak to.

LAURA: Who's that?

JAMES: He's a local delivery man. He's got family in the north. Says his village has been attacked by rebels and he wants to get back but he hasn't got any money for petrol.

LAURA: You thinking what I'm thinking?

JAMES: Yeah. We could help him – and help ourselves at the same time.

LAURA: Isn't the north supposed to be out of bounds? Too dangerous?

JAMES: I guess it's what you call a necessary risk.

LAURA: I thought you were against risks?

JAMES: Yeah, I am. I took precautions.

LAURA: How come?

JAMES: I called a mate of mine. He's a major with the army up there. He'll give us some protection.

LAURA: Won't old Irons contact him?

JAMES: No. He's too concerned with his photo opportunity in Sirghiz. We're yesterday's news, too.

LAURA: Lead the way. We've got a van to catch.

LAURA and JAMES exit.

Teacher's notes

The news according to Ben

Citizenship: *Knowledge, skills and understanding 1g, 1h*

The play is designed to explore, in a light-hearted way, some of the key issues facing news-makers, in particular how news stories are selected, and the process by which priorities are chosen. It also touches on the range of stories covered by news, and to what extent celebrity and showbiz news has a place. Finally, the fact that there is a rival channel … albeit a personal one … raises the issue of the free market and of choice for the viewer.

1) The play

Why does Ben have to cut short his news bulletin? Why does this anger his sister?

What changes do Joe and Holly insist on if they are going to remain working for Ben's channel?

2) General issues

Discuss with students the general differences in the types of news stories covered by, for example, the BBC ten o'clock news, a local commercial radio station morning bulletin, and Radio 5 Live news.

Research has shown that, over recent years, the proportion of international news coverage on television has dropped quite significantly (notwithstanding 11 September and the second Gulf War). Why do students think this is: dumbing down (greater interest in celebrities), the cost of overseas news coverage?

3) Writing

Following Ben's style at the start of the play, ask students to write five headlines about their own life and that of friends and family over the last week or so. Then prioritise the stories and put them in order. Finally, they should write one of the stories in detail, in the style of a news presenter. They can add an on-the-scene reporter if they wish.

Without you

Citizenship: *Knowledge, skills and understanding 1g, 1h*

The play looks at what life might be like in one household if the televisions were removed, but it also touches on several other issues such as the way parents make decisions for the good of the family, as they see it, and the way in which television pervades not just living space, but thinking space, too. In the play, Ricky's mother is seen as the force of common sense.

1) **The play**

   What are Ricky's father's apparent reasons for removing the televisions?

   How does Ricky's mother resolve the issue?

2) **General issues**

   What effect do students think removing the television/s would have in their house? Can they see any benefits?

   What positive effects does television have? Would Ricky's mother's solution – of having TV-free days or nights – work?

3) **Writing**

   Ask students to write a brief summary of the advantages and disadvantages of having televisions in the home, ending with a conclusion saying whether television is ultimately a good or a bad thing.

Happy 24

Citizenship: *Knowledge, skills and understanding 1h*

This relatively short two-hander is designed to raise questions about the nature of the news and our desire to read or hear about bad news, rather than good news. Famously, newscaster Martyn Lewis complained about the lack of good news on television. This play asks the question: would anybody watch it?

At the same time, the issue of *schadenfreude* is touched on: namely the way in which we feel better about ourselves by hearing of the downfall or misfortune of others. The play is deliberately stylised, and designed to be unrealistic in tone and setting.

1) The play

The good news ranges from the enormous and universal, to the local and relatively unimportant. What examples of these two types of news are given? Would students ever find these in the same news bulletin?

Which is more likely to happen in real life: the good news or the bad news version?

2) General issues

Do news stations have a duty to report *all* bad or upsetting news? Is there any news that should not be reported? Ask students to think about war news – is everything shown?

3) Writing

Ask students to write their own made-up 'good' news. There should be at least five items, and they can be as ridiculous as they want. Then try writing the opposite stories: the same subjects, but as bad news.

Island retreat

Citizenship: *Knowledge, skills and understanding 1a, 1h*

This play looks at the rights people have to privacy, and in particular the rights celebrities have. What does the 'public interest' mean? It also explores the underhand tactics used by reporters and photographers in order to get a story. To raise these issues, the play deliberately stereotypes the unscrupulous reporter and photographer, and the pop-star battling addiction. How much does the pop-star need the press, and to what extent is she to blame for having hired a manager, David, to raise her profile? Perhaps he is just doing his job.

1) The play

What two things are of interest to the tabloids about Tamsin's island holiday?

Do students think Tamsin should have done the interview set up by David?

2) General issues

Discuss the dangers and advantages of a privacy law (we don't currently have one, as such, in this country). Students might wish to consider freedom of speech and whether a privacy law would enable powerful and rich people to protect themselves from public scrutiny.

To what extent can celebrities' private lives be considered news? Do countries other than the UK have such a focus on celebrity in their national papers?

3) Writing

Ask students, in groups, to list all the news stories they can remember from the past week – either 'serious' news (political, international etc) or celebrity news. Where did this news come from? Magazines? *Newsround*? *News at Ten*? Share the stories. Were there any stories that all the class had heard? Were they showbiz/celebrity related, or of national/international significance?

Gotta have faith

Citizenship: *Knowledge, skills and understanding 1a, 1b, 1h*

This play concerns a black music group who have eschewed violent and confrontational lyrics. Coming from a faith background, they find themselves facing a choice when they get the chance of a record deal. Several members of the band reject the association of black music with guns and sexist attitudes. Others feel more relaxed about it.

The play raises issues about ethnic identity, but also about how messages are conveyed through dress and music. As a counterpoint to this, the question of whether music actually has any effect – or changes anything – is also raised. These questions are left unanswered, in order that students can explore them themselves.

1) The play

Which member of the group is most unsure about signing up to DubGold?

What argument does Sonia use towards the end of the play when Alvin says that music doesn't change anything, and that the audience doesn't really care?

2) General issues

Are Sonia and Sindy right to object to the way the record company want to promote them, or are they just being naïve? After all, if they want to be a success, don't they have to play by the rules of the game?

Are there certain things that it is unacceptable for singers and songwriters to say or convey, or does everyone have a right to say what they want? Does it make any difference that the opinions are expressed to the background of music rather than, for example, in a newspaper or a book?

3) Writing

Students should write a letter from Jermaine and the other boys trying to persuade Sonia and Sindy to rejoin the band. What arguments might they use to persuade them? (Could the band, for example, do one record with DubGold and then when they were well known, switch to a more 'moral' label?)

Sherry darling

Citizenship: *Knowledge, skills and understanding 1h*

This light-hearted play looks at the way media products convey certain images and messages. By taking the promotion of sherry, traditionally a drink associated with older people, the play opens up the issues of stereotyping in adverts, but also the way in which conventions can be turned on their heads – a common approach in advertising. It might be helpful to make reference to other adverts that have reinvented a product in some way. Most famously, Skoda cars have tried to rid themselves of the image that they were shoddy and unfashionable. Have they succeeded?

1) The play

What is the first idea Zach comes up with for advertising sherry?

Would the idea he and Louise presented to Mr Hawksey have actually worked? What disadvantages – apart from being sued – would there be to using someone else's idea and slogan?

2) General issues

Advertising conveys strong messages about people, places and products. Pick a well known alcoholic drink advertised on television. Discuss what happens in the advert, and what this conveys about the drink or, more importantly, the people who drink it.

Advertisers (for example tobacco companies) have often claimed that adverts don't make people buy a product, but they do encourage them to buy a particular brand. In other words, they would buy cars anyway, but the advert suggests a particular make of car. Do students agree? Or do they think adverts actually make people buy things they wouldn't have considered otherwise?

3) Writing

Students should create their own magazine advert for Hawksey's Sherry to suggest that the drink is hip and trendy. They mustn't use the slogan 'Dare to be different', but should come up with their own.

The truth about Gina

Citizenship: *Knowledge, skills and understanding 1a, 1g, 1h*

This play has a serious message and a serious tone to it throughout, raising some key questions. How can we trust what we are told? What is the truth about someone, and should we conceal the truth to protect the feelings of others? Are the press right to pursue a story at all costs?

The play also covers a number of other issues: how a school handles bereavement, and how it handles the press. It also touches upon the effects of bullying, and the way things can escalate. It ends without an answer to the question: what is the truth? Students may wish to consider whether anyone, even the headteacher, has the full story.

The play needs to be approached sensitively as it deals with the death of a student, and teachers may wish to take some time to prepare students in advance for the subject matter. Finally, although most of the play is intended to be realistic in tone, the last scene is deliberately stylised and should be performed almost like a dream, or chant.

1) The play

How does the newspaper front page report Gina's death?

Do students approve of the reporter's methods for getting a story from the students at the school?

What assumption does Sam make when he visits the newspaper's offices?

2) General issues

Do newspapers have a duty to give everyone's perspective when a serious event happens? Is this possible? Or do papers always have to have a viewpoint? In fact, is it ever possible to write a fair story?

How do students think the headteacher handles the situation? Would they have done things differently?

3) Writing

Students should write the speech the headteacher is about to give about Gina and what really happened, then compare what they have written with a friend. Did they all arrive at the same conclusion? If not, what does this show?

The first casualty

Citizenship: *Knowledge, skills and understanding 1g, 1h, 1i*

The play takes place in a country that could be Iraq, although the names of the place (Sirghiz) and the people concerned are deliberately fictional.

The play focuses on the issue of the press being embedded in the military (i.e. protected by, and fed news by, the military) as opposed to being free to report what they want, but exposed perhaps to greater risk to their lives.

How important is it that the press are loyal to home forces? If the conflict is considered a 'good thing' (e.g. removing an evil dictator), should the press be allowed to hamper the forces of good – if they are, indeed, good?

The play tries to present the press in a more favourable light than some of the earlier pieces, and to avoid some of the stereotyping of the more humorous dramas.

1) The play

General Irons uses a range of expressions that suggest that the allied forces are on the side of good. He also avoids using words such as 'killed'. What specific choices of words and phrases does he use to show the military action in a good light?

Why do Laura and James lose their protection from the military? How do they plan to cover a future news story?

2) General issues

The phrase 'the first casualty of war is truth' has been used many times. Ask students what role they think the press should play during wartime? What would have happened in World War 2 had people been fully aware, at the start of the war, how badly things were going?

3) Writing

Ask students to file Laura and James' report about what happened to them in Sirghiz. It should include what actually happened (e.g. the attack on Laura) and what they were told about Sirghiz both before and after their trip.